My Grandmother's name is

_____

But I call her

_____

This book belongs to her

DEAR GRANDMA

by dolli tingle

The C. R. Gibson Company
Norwalk, Connecticut

I love my Grandma,
Yes, I do.
She's the one I hurry to.
When things go wrong
I know that she
Will almost always
Side with me.

DEAR GRANDMA

This special book for you is from

Paste Photo
here

Name_____

Parents_____

Date picture was taken

_____

When Grandma is my sitter
She tells stories that are nifty.
She remembers olden days
Like even nineteen fifty.
I may get a little sleepy
But I've got it through my head,
As long as she keeps talking
I don't have to go to bed.

I try hard to be polite.
I do everything just right
When my Grandma takes me out
For lunch or tea.
I don't slump, I sit up straight
And I even clean my plate.
I'm so good I really can't
Believe it's me!

I measured me with a ruler,
I found out how much I weigh,
I counted up all my birthdays
And I wrote down the date today.

Now all you have to do is look
To read about me in this book.

DEAR GRANDMA

Here's the latest news about me

My nickname is

_____

Age _____

Weight _____

Height _____

Color eyes _____

Color hair _____

Date _____

Who laughs and giggles
At my jokes?
Who is it I don't have to coax
To play, as I do other folks?
My Grandma!

Who cheers me
When I'm sad and blue?
Who can I tell my troubles to?
Who really listens
When I do?

My Grandma!

There's nobody like a Grandma
To appreciate your worth.
My Grandma thinks my pictures
Make the greatest show on earth.

DEAR GRANDMA

Here is a picture I made for you

I hope you like it

My Grandma likes to buy me things.
She showers me with presents.
Dad says she thinks I'm royalty
Set down amongst the peasants!

My Grandma's cookies
Are the best.
Nobody else can beat 'em.
The only problem is my Mom
Who seldom lets me eat 'em.

I'm growing fast
And what I liked last year
Is now passé.
Mom says she can't keep up with me,
I change from day to day.
So, Grandma, here's a list I made
To keep you up to date
On things I think are super
And on stuff I really hate.

My favorite things right now

Toy _____

Story _____

Animal _____

Food _____

Song _____

And some things I DON'T LIKE

_____

_____

_____

When other Grandmas start to brag,
My Grandma opens up her bag
And, faster than the speed of light,
She shows 'em snapshots left and
    right.
She tells who's who and where and
    when
And how and why and back again.
I wouldn't say that she's a bore
But no one ever yells "Encore!"

We take such beautiful pictures
According to Mommy and Dad,
That we could be making a fortune
Just posing like this for an ad.

DEAR GRANDMA

Here is a photograph for you

Paste Photo
here

Date when photo was taken

_____

Where_____